PAUL GEORGE

NBA STAR

By Douglas Lynne

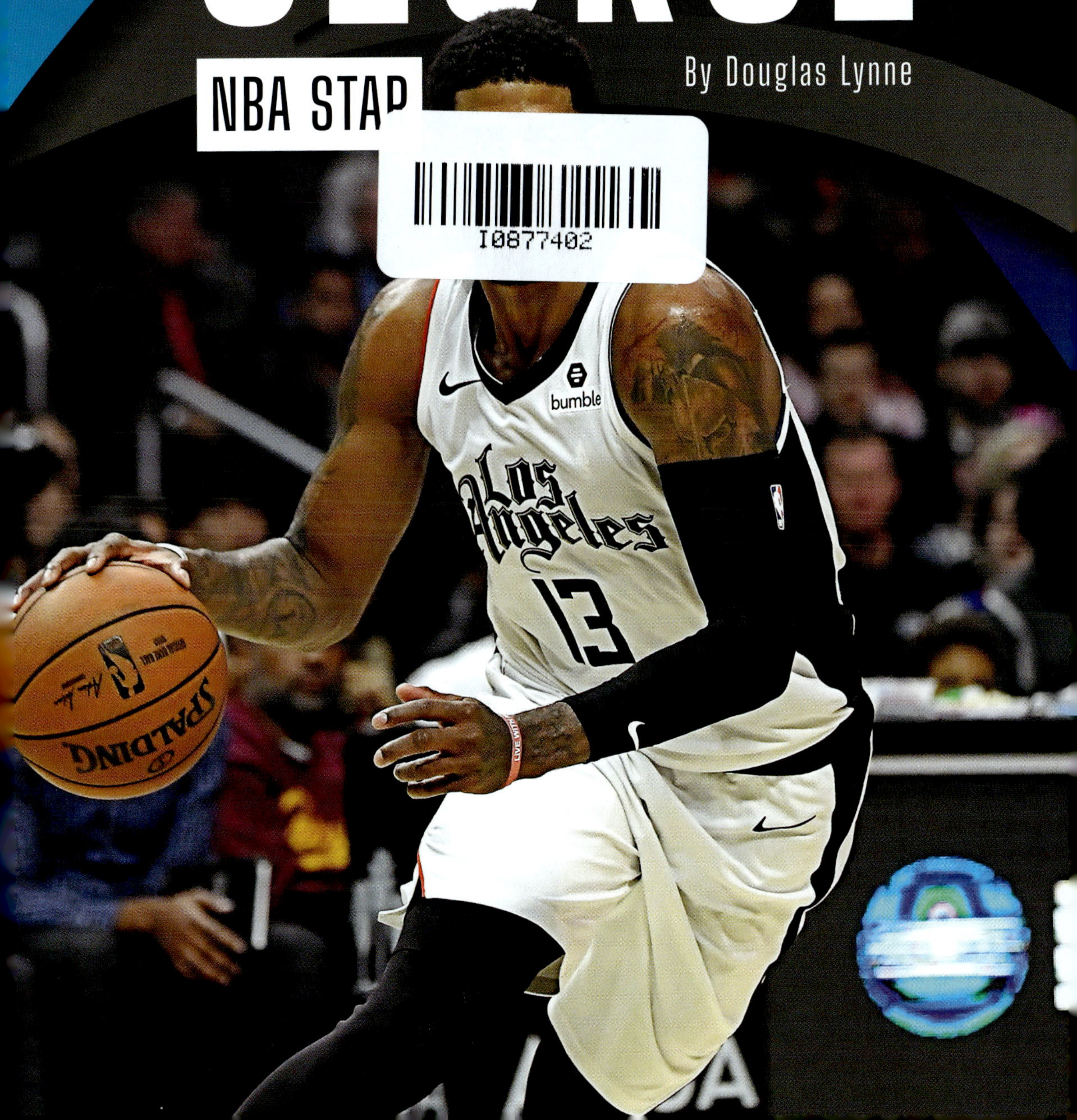

Book design by Christine Ha
Cover design by Jake Nordby

Photographs ©: Mark J. Terrill/AP Images, cover, 1; Kelvin Kuo/AP Images, 4, 7, 8, 23; iStockphoto, 10; Andy Cripe/The Gazette Times/AP Images, 12; Michael Conroy/AP Images, 14; Shutterstock Images, 16; Sue Ogroki/AP Images, 19; Brian Rothmuller/Icon Sportswire/AP Images, 20; Red Line Editorial, 22

Press Box Books, an imprint of Press Room Editions.

Library of Congress Control Number: 2020901594

ISBN
978-1-63494-219-5 (library bound)
978-1-63494-237-9 (paperback)
978-1-63494-255-3 (epub)
978-1-63494-273-7 (hosted ebook)

Distributed by North Star Editions, Inc.
2297 Waters Drive
Mendota Heights, MN 55120
www.northstareditions.com

Printed in the United States of America
082020

ABOUT THE AUTHOR

Douglas Lynne is a freelance writer. He spent many years working in the media, first in newspapers and later for online organizations, covering everything from breaking news to politics to entertainment to sports. He lives in Minneapolis, Minnesota.

TABLE OF CONTENTS

bumble
CLIPPERS
13

1 THE RIGHT GUY

Paul George ran up the court on a fast break. Los Angeles Clippers teammate Lou Williams sent a pass his way. A New Orleans Pelicans defender stood between George and the hoop. No problem. George stepped back for a fadeaway jumper. The ball bounced off the backboard and into the basket.

The Clippers had high hopes for George. They had traded for the All-Star

Paul George went home to play for the Clippers in 2019.

forward before the 2019–20 season. The team already had one superstar in small forward Kawhi Leonard. Fans hoped George and Leonard could lead the Clippers to their first championship. George showed why in his first game.

The 6′8″ George can do it all. His fadeaway basket against New Orleans was only the beginning. The Pelicans often unleashed two defenders to try to stop George. It hardly mattered. He was able to post up against smaller players. Then he'd turn around and nail a jumper. Other times he'd step back and hit a three-pointer.

In just 24 minutes, George scored 33 points. He did so despite taking just 17 shots. Three of his baskets were three-pointers. And he went 10-for-10 on free throws on the night.

George has long been one of the NBA's best shooters.

George also takes pride in other parts of his game, such as passing.

What makes George special, however, is that he does much more than score points. He displayed his strong dribbling and passing skills against the Pelicans. When he didn't have the ball, George knew just where to be. He'd position himself to block the path of a defender. This opened space for his teammates. George also is a fierce defender. He ended the game with nine rebounds and four assists.

A NEW CLIPPERS ERA

The Clippers arrived in Los Angeles in 1984. They have long been overshadowed by their neighbors, the Lakers. It didn't help that the Clippers were often a losing team. A new era began in 2019–20, though. Kawhi Leonard was the defending NBA Finals Most Valuable Player (MVP). He announced in July he was signing with the Clippers. Then the team announced it had traded for George, too.

George is a dynamic, two-way star. He had proven that over nine National Basketball Association (NBA) seasons. Now, playing with his hometown Clippers, he appeared ready to take the next step.

Palmdale
CITY LIMIT
POP 152,750 ELEV 2,659
EMERGENCY - CALL 9-1-1

THE PRIDE OF PALMDALE 2

Paul George was born on May 2, 1990. He grew up in Palmdale, California. Though his hometown was just north of Los Angeles, it felt far from the bright lights of Hollywood. Many families were working class, including Paul's. His dad worked in an auto parts shop. His mom took care of the home.

Paul was a shy kid. There wasn't a lot for him to do around town, either.

Palmdale, California, is far removed from the big-city feel of Los Angeles.

Paul throws down a dunk for Fresno State in 2009.

So he spent a lot of time playing basketball with his older sisters. He was pretty good. But it wasn't until later in high school that Paul became a star. His athletic dunks wowed fans. But he worked hard to develop an accurate shot, too. So even though he was tall, he could score from all over the court.

The biggest colleges didn't think Paul was good enough. So he wound up at nearby Fresno State University. The team played in a smaller conference. But Paul showed rare skill for a player his size. After two years, he decided to go pro. The Indiana Pacers picked him 10th in the 2010 NBA Draft.

STAR SISTERS

Paul's older sisters were great athletes, too. Teiosha went on to play basketball at Pepperdine University. Portala's sport was volleyball. She played at the Division II level in college. The George kids were competitive growing up. Paul learned a lot about basketball from Teiosha. She also taught him to be tough.

PORTLAN
PACERS
24

A LONG ROAD HOME

3

George showed flashes of greatness early on with the Pacers. By his third season, in 2012–13, he was ready to break out. George averaged 17.4 points, 7.6 rebounds, and 4.1 assists that year. He also made his first All-Star Game.

Behind George, the Pacers went 56–26 the next year. And for the second season in a row, they advanced to the Eastern Conference Finals. George stepped up

George became a star with the Indiana Pacers.

George overcame a devastating injury to play for Team USA in the 2016 Olympics.

his game in the series against LeBron James and the Miami Heat. In one game, he made eight of 10 shots in the fourth quarter. Indiana ended up losing the series, but George's future looked bright.

That summer, George was selected to play on the US national team. The Olympics were two years away, but if George played well for Team USA, he'd likely be part of the roster. However, before he could even get started, disaster struck.

During a scrimmage in Las Vegas in August 2014, George jumped to block a shot. When he landed, his right foot came down on the base of the basket. Both bones

OLYMPIC CHAMP

Even after his devastating leg injury, George came back to play with Team USA at the 2016 Olympics. He started two of eight games for the US team in Rio de Janeiro, Brazil. As usual, he contributed all over the court. His play helped Team USA win the gold medal.

in his lower leg snapped. It was a gruesome injury. Some wondered if he would ever be the same player.

George missed all but the final six games of the Pacers' next season. But before long, he was playing as well as ever. He was named the NBA Comeback Player of the Year in 2015–16.

George had become one of the NBA's best players. But the Pacers knew he wanted to play closer to home. The team didn't want him to simply walk away. So before his contract ended, Indiana traded him. George joined the Oklahoma City Thunder in the summer of 2017.

Oklahoma was still far from his home in California. But Thunder officials hoped he'd like playing there and decide to stay. And that's what happened. George had enjoyed a great season playing alongside star point guard

George had two excellent seasons with the Oklahoma City Thunder.

Russell Westbrook. So following the 2018–19 season, he agreed to a new four-year deal.

George appeared to be comfortable in Oklahoma City. He was at his all-around best in 2018–19. He averaged 28.0 points and 8.2 rebounds per game. Both were career highs.

George (13) and Leonard were a big part of the Clippers' future plans.

And he finished third in the league MVP voting. Then, suddenly, he was gone.

The Los Angeles Clippers were looking to make big changes. They wanted George to be a part of their future. So in the summer of 2019, George finally went home as part of a blockbuster trade.

In Los Angeles, George teamed with forward Kawhi Leonard, who had led the Toronto Raptors to the NBA title a year earlier. Together, they made the Clippers a force in the NBA Western Conference. George shot 40 percent from three-point range and was second on the team in scoring. He and Leonard were ready to help the Clippers win their first NBA title.

TIMELINE MAP

1. **Palmdale, California: 1990**
   Paul George is born on May 2.
2. **Fresno, California: 2009–10**
   George averages 16.8 points, 7.2 rebounds, 3.0 assists, 2.2 steals, and 0.8 blocks per game as a sophomore at Fresno State.
3. **New York, New York: 2010**
   The Indiana Pacers select George with the 10th pick in the NBA Draft on June 24.
4. **San Antonio, Texas: 2010**
   George makes his NBA debut for the Pacers on October 27, scoring four points off the bench.
5. **Indianapolis, Indiana: 2014**
   George scores 37 points as the Pacers beat the Miami Heat in Game 5 of the Eastern Conference Finals on May 28.
6. **Las Vegas, Nevada: 2014**
   George breaks his right leg playing with Team USA on August 1.
7. **Rio de Janeiro, Brazil: 2016**
   George helps Team USA win the gold medal at the Rio Olympics.
8. **Oklahoma City, Oklahoma: 2017**
   On October 19 George scores 28 points in his first game with the Oklahoma City Thunder.
9. **Los Angeles, California: 2019**
   The Clippers complete a blockbuster trade on July 10 to unite George with the recently signed Kawhi Leonard.

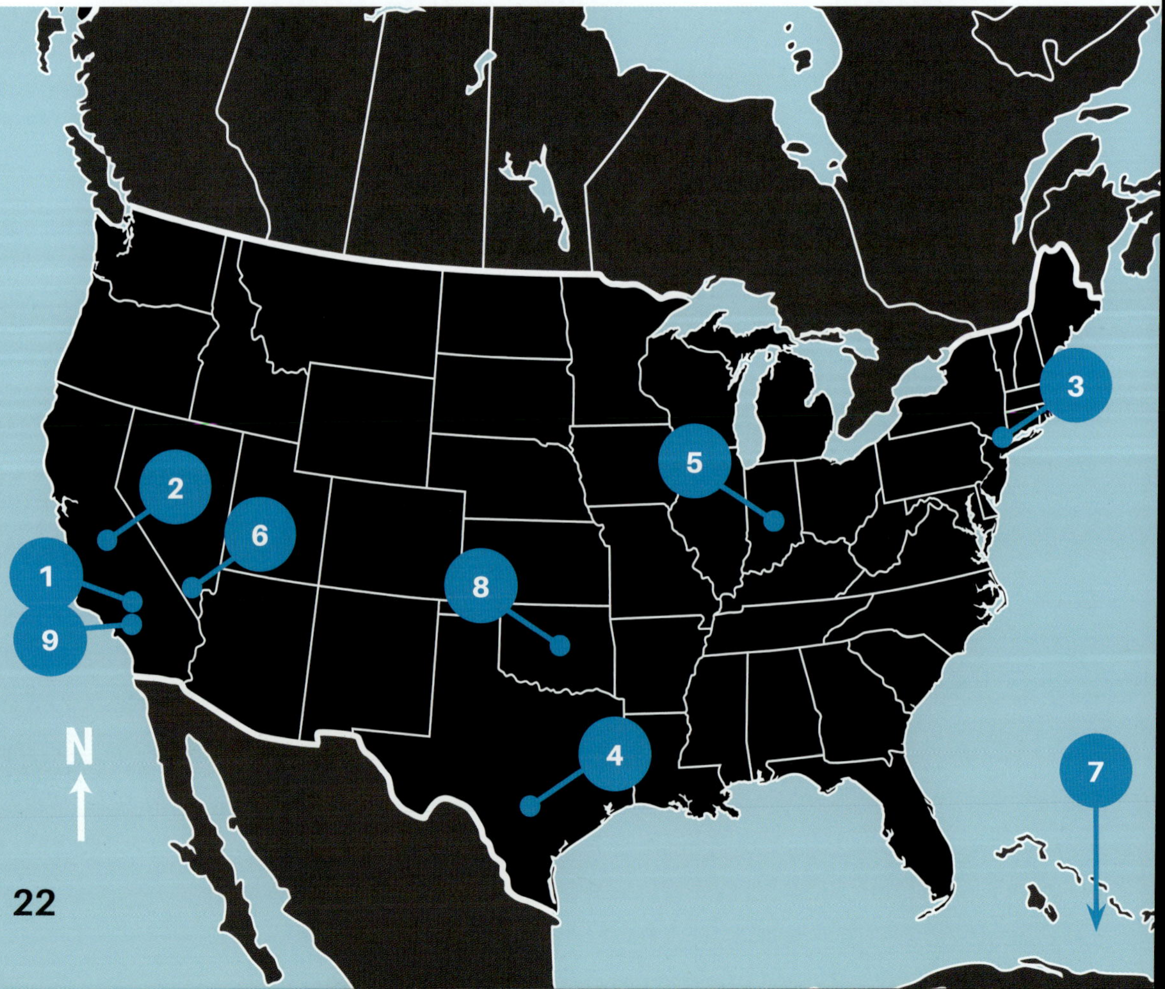

AT-A-GLANCE

PAUL GEORGE

Birth date: May 2, 1990

Birthplace: Palmdale, California

Position: Small forward

Height: 6 feet 8 inches

Weight: 220 pounds

Current team: Los Angeles Clippers (2019–)

Past teams: Fresno State Bulldogs (2008–10), Indiana Pacers (2010–17), Oklahoma City Thunder (2017–19)

Major awards: NBA All-Star (2013, 2014, 2016, 2017, 2018, 2019), NBA Most Improved Player (2013), NBA All-Defensive First Team (2014, 2019), NBA Comeback Player of the Year (2015–16), All-NBA First Team (2019)

Accurate through the 2019–20 season.

MORE INFORMATION

To learn more about Paul George, go to **pressboxbooks.com/AllAccess**.

These links are routinely monitored and updated to provide the most current information available.

GLOSSARY

conference
A group of teams within a sports league.

contract
An agreement between a team and a player.

draft
A system by which sports leagues divide up new talent.

dynamic
Energetic and forceful.

fast break
When a basketball team gains possession of the ball on its own end of the court and quickly moves the ball toward the other basket.

post up
To take a position near the opponent's basket with one's back to the hoop.

INDEX